CHRISTIANITY AND
WESTERN CIVILIZATION

Christianity and Western Civilization

BEING THE RAYMOND FRED WEST MEMORIAL LECTURES
AT STANFORD UNIVERSITY
APRIL 5–7, 1954

By CARLTON J. H. HAYES

Seth Low Professor Emeritus of History in Columbia University

STANFORD UNIVERSITY PRESS
Stanford, California
London: Geoffrey Cumberlege
Oxford University Press

STANFORD UNIVERSITY PRESS, STANFORD, CALIFORNIA

Published in Great Britain, India, and Pakistan by Geoffrey Cumberlege,
Oxford University Press, London, Bombay, and Karachi

The Baker and Tayor Company, Hillside, New Jersey
Henry M. Snyder & Company, Inc., 440 Fourth Avenue, New York 16
W. S. Hall & Company, 457 Madison Avenue, New York 22

Prefatory Note

To Stanford University I am grateful for inviting me to deliver on its beautiful campus this year the Raymond Fred West Memorial Lectures, and for making it the occasion for doing honor to the motto under which Columbia University is simultaneously celebrating its bicentennial— which incidentally happens to be the semicentennial of my own graduation from Columbia. The motto, "Man's right to knowledge and the free use thereof," does neatly express the governing principle not only of Columbia but of Stanford and all the other great institutions of higher learning throughout the free world. Freedom in education is indeed a heritage and a crown of our Western civilization. It must be upheld and advanced if this historic civilization is to remain the source and citadel of freedom.

In the lectures, which are here published practically verbatim, my purpose has been to set forth a thesis that certain distinctive features of Western civilization, specifically its ideals of freedom, limited government, and humanitarian compassion, have been inspired and given substance primarily by its historic religion. I appreciate that in three summary lectures it is impossible adequately to develop and support the thesis. I can only hope that what is here said in cursory and generalized fashion may serve to stimulate broader and deeper reflection on the abiding sig-

v

nificance of Christianity to Western civilization and to whatever world civilization may now be in the making.

Most of the Biblical quotations in the following pages, I should add, are from the recent English translation by Monsignor Ronald Knox.

C. J. H. H.

AFTON, NEW YORK
Easter Sunday, 1954

Table of Contents

CHRISTIANITY AND
WESTERN CIVILIZATION

Introduction

1

IN THE present perplexing times, amid what seems to be the gravest crisis in world affairs, an extraordinarily large amount of discussion goes on, mainly of a pessimistic nature, about our historic Western civilization. Is it worth preserving, we are asked, or has it outlived its usefulness? Isn't it already in decline and decay, and aren't its traditional ideals being supplanted and rendered obsolete by the "realities" latterly thrust upon us by the materialistic philosophy of Marx, the subconscious psychology of Freud, and the skeptical existentialism of Sartre? Above all, isn't our Western civilization a puny, partial, and passing thing in comparison with the World civilization which the spread of technology promises for the future?

Of all such discussion, I must say I take a very dim view. Into it I shall enter, in the present chapters, only incidentally. Being a historian and not a prophet or soothsayer, I make no pretense of knowing what the future holds in store for us. Being naturally of an optimistic and sanguine temperament, I have scant sympathy with contemporary criers of doom. I unblushingly persist in believing that our Western civilization has long been and still is a great liberal and progressive civilization—the greatest the world has ever produced—and that, having survived other troubled ages, it is likely to survive the present one.

This depends primarily, it seems to me, on whether our civilization retains its association with, and continues to draw inspiration from, the historic religion of the West, or whether, by substituting new gods for old, it is subverted and transformed. Although association of a civilization or culture with a particular religion is commonplace with anthropologists and with such philosophers of history as Arnold Toynbee and Christopher Dawson, it is surprisingly ignored or lost sight of by most popular commentators on the world scene of today. I shall try in the present discussion to turn the limelight on one phase of it: the historic relationship to our Western civilization of Judaeo-Graeco-Christianity, Catholic and Protestant.

2

Human beings are human beings, the world over, and all have a like human nature. As animals, they are born; they eat and sleep and procreate; they die. Unlike other animals, they mature very slowly and undergo a lengthy period of being cared for and indoctrinated by their elders. Endowed, moreover, with greater mental power, they are peculiarly educable, and as such capable of absorbing a vast deal of accumulated knowledge—linguistic, cultural, technological. No man is entirely self-made. Every man is mainly a product of his ancestry and environment, and of history.

Nevertheless, while human nature everywhere remains essentially the same, the civilizing of mankind—that is, its education and indoctrination—has followed no uniform pattern nor produced any uniform content. Rather, long-standing differences of environment and historical development have served to establish among men a variety of cultures and civilizations.

An American or West European who resides, even briefly, in the Far East, or in India, or in the Middle and Near East, becomes quickly aware of contrasts between the civilizations of those areas and the civilization with which he is familiar at home. There are different traditions, different attitudes toward life. There are different manners and customs, different standards and values of conduct, different art forms, different meanings of words.

To an appreciable extent, cultural differences obtain within the area of our Western civilization, say between Scandinavians and Spaniards, between Italians and Englishmen, between Germans and Frenchmen, between West Europeans and Americans, between North and South Americans. But such differences are slight in comparison with cultural differences between any of these peoples and those of the East. Despite diversity of language and nationality, despite local peculiarities, all of western and central Europe, all of America and Australasia, and scattered outposts elsewhere, share in a common distinctive civilization—that of the West, centrally of what in modern times we call the Atlantic Community. An experienced and thoughtful traveler from one country to another within this community will find more that is familiar in thought and behavior than what is strange. He will be more intellectually "at home" than he would be if traveling outside the West.

It is frequently assumed that the most basic characteristic of our Western civilization is material: its scientific nature, its technology, its "know-how," its mass production of goods. Whence is drawn the conclusion that the contemporary spread of industrialization from West to East will assure the spread of like ideas and attitudes and behavior patterns everywhere, and will thus create, in the not too distant future, a common global civilization, a truly One World.

I, for one, question both the assumption and the conclusion. I recognize, of course, that within the last half century material features of our Western civilization have been increasingly superimposed on other civilizations all over the world. Networks of railways and airlines now exist throughout the Far East and in India, for example, as well as in Europe and America, and so do factories and foundries and mechanical exploitation of natural resources, and radios and a variety of electrical gadgets, even Ritz-like or Hilton-like hotels. I also recognize the logic in the proposition that *if* every civilization is based on, and determined by, strictly economic and material conditions, then world-wide adoption of modern technology and mechanized production should, and indeed must, eventuate in a real and fairly uniform world civilization. But the "if," in my opinion, is a big "if."

It should be borne in mind, I think, that the spreading industrialization of the present day is a relatively recent phenomenon, not only outside but inside the area of Western civilization. Its main development in the West is hardly more than a century old. And everywhere it has been too brief to warrant any certain prophecy about its ability to fuse different civilizations into one. Perhaps, given time enough, it will affect all mankind in like manner and with like results, but only then, I suspect, if it is accompanied by universally accepted religion.

Man, I submit, has never lived by bread alone, and, human nature being what it is, he probably never will. For him modern industrialization, like any earlier way of earning bread, is only one aspect of his civilization. Wherever the new technology penetrates, it adds to, but does not necessarily subtract from, much older and more deeply implanted habits and ideals of existing civilization.

Japan was the first country outside the Atlantic Community to be extensively Westernized, in the sense of being industrialized, but, as is generally recognized, Japan's basic civilization has not thereby become just like ours; it remains essentially what it has long been, Far Eastern. Similarly, no country, except England, has been so quickly and intensively industrialized as Soviet Russia, and yet both the methods employed and the outcome have tended to harmonize with older and deeper traditions: in the case of Russia, with the despotism of East European Byzantine civilization; in the case of England, with the liberty of Western civilization. In fine, history seems clearly to indicate from earliest times of which we have record that the borrowing of material inventions by one civilization from another, say of the plow or the boat, of paper or firearms, or latterly of the automobile or the radio, has been normal and usual but has hardly had destructive effect on the borrowing civilization.

I do not deny the existence or an importance of material factors in civilization or a part they may play in altering it. What I do assert is that they are not so basic or so distinguishing as spiritual religious factors. A distinctive historic religion is certainly a mark of the area of a distinctive civilization, and a chief fashioner of the ideals and behavior patterns of the peoples of that area, a potent conditioner of their economy, politics, art, and intellectual life. One simply cannot understand Far Eastern civilization without its setting in Buddhism and Confucianism, or Middle Eastern civilization without its Moslem background. The distinctive civilization of India is interwoven with Hinduism, and that of Eastern Europe with Eastern Orthodoxy. It is likewise with our Western civilization, which could not be what it is without its having been fostered by Western Christianity. This Christianity is the common heritage of all the lands and peoples that make up the Atlantic Community and the Western world.

Not everybody in the Western world is a professed or conscious Christian, and many professed Christians fall far short of realizing Christian ideals. Especially within the last century there has been, throughout the West, a big growth in the number of intellectuals, and of workmen and farmers, who reject or ignore the Christian religion and who seldom if ever enter a Christian church. Yet the mores which emanate from historic religious belief always outlast the belief; and to this generalization our Western world furnishes no exception. For none of us, whether we are practicing Christians or not, can quite rid ourselves of customs and sanctions which derive from historic Christianity.

Sunday remains a special day for all of us, whether we go to church or play golf. We all know of the Bible, whether we read it or not. Most of us send out greeting cards at Christmas and dress up at Easter. Our laws and law courts have Christian overtones; and the Ten Commandments and the Golden Rule, though very often violated, are still counsels of perfection for millions throughout the West, outside as well as inside the churches.

3

There are many respects in which Christianity has influenced and helped to shape our historic Western civilization. That is obviously true of most of our social usages and customs, and of our literature and art. Surely the Christian Bible has been for centuries *the great* book of the West, and in such translations as the Latin Vulgate, the German of Luther's, and the English of the King James version, it has been read and quoted as no other book; its latest English translations, whether the revised versions in America or that of Ronald Knox in Britain, are current best sellers. And think how thoroughly impregnated with Christian tradition is so much of the West's vernacular literature, from Dante and Chaucer down through Shakespeare and Cervantes, Milton and Bunyan, Scott and Tennyson, to Gerard Hopkins and Paul Claudel, T. S. Eliot and Graham Greene. It is likewise with so much of our historic architecture, painting, and sculpture, and with the West's distinctive music from plain song and hymnology to masterpieces of Palestrina, Bach, Mozart, and Beethoven.

Important as are these cultural features of Western civilization, I shall not attempt to treat of them in the present discussion. Rather, I shall here concentrate on certain other features which have historically been influenced by Christianity and which have crucial significance in our age. First is the West's peculiar emphasis on individuality and liberty. Second, closely linked to the first, is the West's chronic repugnance to unlimited authority and its preference for plural and constitutional government. Third is the West's progressive character, coupled with broadening application of its ideal of compassion.

In relating these features of our Western civilization to the prevalent religion of the West, I do not wish to be understood as maintaining that Christianity has been their sole fashioner. I readily concede the concomitant influence of political, economic, and intellectual developments of a non-Christian sort. If I seem to overstress the religious influence, it is because I am seeking to correct an obscurantist understressing of it in recent times.

Nor, when I talk about Christianity, am I unmindful of its roots in Judaism and its cross-fertilization by ancient Graeco-Roman thought and culture. Western civilization, I know well, did not originate in Bethlehem or Nazareth. Elements of it appeared many centuries B.C., and the religious transformation it eventually underwent was through a Christianity which, along with distinctive teachings of its own, held in high esteem both Jewish prophets and Greek philosophers. It is Judaeo-Graeco-Christianity, let me emphasize, which for nineteen centuries has been the prevailing religion of the West.

One other caveat I would enter, before proceeding with the main topics. One should not infer from what I casually say about other religions and other civilizations that I have any thought of belittling them. Because Islam or Buddhism or Hinduism has not served to inspire the particular features of Western civilization with which I am dealing, it does not follow that those religions have failed to make major contributions to the important historic civilizations respectively of Near and Middle East, of Far East, and of India. I merely mean, in any reference to them, to suggest that they are different from Christianity and that their influence on certain aspects of civilization has been different.

I. *Individuality and Liberty*

1

LET US now turn to discussion of particular topics. I begin with individuality and liberty. These concepts, as most Americans and West Europeans understand and apply them, are not only fundamental but peculiar to the West. Elsewhere they have been an exotic, hothouse transplant. They have had no deep roots or perennial fruitage in Asia or Africa or in Russia.

The importance of the individual—of each individual—was extolled by ancient Jewish prophets and Greek and Roman Stoics, but it received its chief sanction and abiding significance in Western civilization from the West's religious faith in Christianity. For Christianity's prime and most distinctive doctrines were those of the Incarnation and the Resurrection, with human implications in each, that just as God became man in the person of Christ, so man might have fellowship in his Godhead; that just as the God-Man rose from the dead, so too would the human being. And human individuality would continue beyond the grave, without its being of the shadowy sort depicted by pagan philosophers and poets, or involving the idea of transmigration into other animals as entertained in India.

From these fundamental Christian doctrines of the Incarnation and Resurrection has been naturally and logically derived the West's idea of the dignity and worth of each and every human being. If more were needed to exalt man, it has been supplied by the further Christian doctrine of man's being a rational creature endowed with sufficiently free will to enable him to choose between good and evil, between heaven and hell. As a Catholic poet, Francis Thompson, puts it:

> *There is no expeditious road*
> *To pack and label men for God,*
> *And save them by the barrel-load.*

Which means, of course, that salvation, for the Christian, is not a mass affair but an affair of the individual.

According to the Gospel narratives which have come down to us, Jesus Christ does not seem to have been immediately concerned with any mass movement or any program of social reform. He proclaimed no crusade against slavery or class distinctions or poverty. He organized no foundations for international peace or treatment of leprosy or insanity or for research in the physical and social sciences. He gave no evidence of being a nationalist or a socialist.

This is not to say that Christian teaching has not had immense influence in inspiring and shaping such characteristic social movements of Western civilization as abolitionism, pacifism, humanitarianism, nationalism, and socialism. These, however, have been indirect results; to them I shall return in a later chapter. Here let me dwell on Christ's direct and immediate mission. It was obviously a mission of recognizing and dignifying individuality, of sanctifying each person. Reform of the individual was all-important; without it no reform of society, no flowering of the kingdom of God, was possible.

The Gospel narratives teem with examples of Christ's recognition and praise of personal worth and dignity in all kinds of men and women—in carpenters, in fishermen and tavernkeepers, in Roman army officers and alien Samaritans, in men of wealth like Nicodemus and Joseph of Arimathea, in a poor bereaved widow, and a woman taken in adultery, in a contemplative Mary and a housewifely Martha, even in that most unpopular of all men, a tax collector. Nor did he treat these varied personalities as cogs in a machine or objects of laboratory experiment. Each was distinct and different from all the others. Each had at least a measure of free will. Each possessed a sacred individuality.

Individuality, according to Christ, was far from involving the personal egotism with which it was associated by ancient Stoics and Epicureans or by modern Utilitarians. On the contrary, it was humble and infused with compassion and a sense of justice. It was not self-centered, but God-centered. True, the brotherhood of men under the fatherhood of God was an idea antedating Christ. Christ, however, underscored it and qualified it, not only in the Golden Rule, "Do to other men all that you would have them do to you," but also in that other saying, "When you do it to one of the least of my brethren here, you do it to me."

A classic expression of this concept of individuality,

with its corollary of human equality, was supplied by the Apostle Paul in his exhortation to the Christians at Colossae: "You must be quit of the old self, and the habits that went with it; you must be clothed in the new self . . . so that the image of the God who created it is its pattern. Here is no more Gentile and Jew, no more circumcised and uncircumcised; no one is barbarian, or Scythian, no one is slave or free man; there is nothing but Christ in any of us. You are God's chosen people, holy and well-beloved; the livery you wear must be tender compassion, kindness, humility, gentleness, and patience; you must bear with one another's faults, be generous to each other, where somebody has given grounds for complaint; the Lord's generosity to you must be the model of yours. And, to crown all this, charity; that is the bond which makes us perfect."

The Christian concept of individuality was basic to what St. James described as the perfect law of freedom, or liberty, and to what subsequent Christian philosophers associated with "natural rights." The historically important fact about it is that wherever Christianity spread and became deeply enrooted, an ideal of individual liberty arose. Indeed, the ideal has proven a veritable leaven in our Western civilization. Down through the centuries, to be sure, many professed Christians, including statesmen and high-ranking prelates, have been impervious or resistant to it, and it has recurrently been questioned or abused by Western intellectuals. Yet the ideal has constantly remained, raising critics of despotism, inciting to popular rebellion against tyranny, and conditioning social attitudes and behavior.

In the face of Christian precepts of individuality and freedom, our Western civilization has never developed a caste system. It has been characterized, rather, by a remarkable fluidity of classes; a shifting of bondsmen into freemen, of serfs into peasant proprietors, of apprenticed workmen into masters; a varying role, with much interpenetration, of upper and middle and lower classes; and all usually accompanied by a considerable freedom of movement and migration. Nor could the dignity of labor be lost sight of in a civilization the founder of whose religion was a carpenter and the apostolic missionaries of which were fishermen and a tentmaker.

Moreover, women have always enjoyed a greater freedom in our Western civilization than in any other. If they wear veils, they do so of their own accord. If they are theoretically subject to their husbands, they actually, in Christian lands, have commanded armies and ruled over nations. It could hardly be otherwise in a civilization whose religion especially honored a woman as the mother of its God-Man, and whose Roman ritual says of her, quoting Ecclesiasticus,

> *I have been exalted as a cedar in Libanus and as a*
> *cyprus on Mount Sion;*
> *I have been exalted as a palm tree in Cades and*
> *as a rose garden planted in Jericho;*
> *I have been exalted as a splendid olive tree in an*
> *open field,*
> *And I have been exalted as a plane tree by the*
> *water ways along the city streets.*

*I have breathed forth fragrance as of balsam and
    cinnamon;
I have exhaled the sweetness of the choicest myrrh.*

2

The Christian West, as no other part of the world, has
been replete with rebellions against tyranny and affirma-
tions of liberty. The Magna Carta which was extorted in
the Middle Ages from a despotic English king was no excep-
tional document. Similar charters of liberty were wrested
from monarchs or barons in almost every country of western and central Europe. It was then, moreover, that European slavery disappeared and serfdom declined; that monarchy was limited, not only in England by parliament, but
widely on the Continent by diet, estates-general, or cortes;
that the individual was generally assured of trial by jury
and protected against arbitrary arrest; that a degree of economic freedom was acquired by guilds, and of academic
freedom by universities; and that individualistic democracy
prevailed alike in urban communes and in monastic life.

Without that background of freedom in practice as
well as in theory, the further later development of personal
liberty could hardly have taken place. The British up-
heavals of the seventeenth century, starting with the Puritan revolt and eventuating in the "Glorious Revolution"
and the "Declaration of Rights" of 1689, were led by
ardent Christians and were defended, both at home and in
America, on the ground that they ensured the immemorial
natural rights of individual Englishmen. And the classic
exposition of this idea by John Locke at the close of the

seventeenth century proved a powerful factor in confirming liberal doctrine across the Atlantic and re-enforcing it across the English Channel on the European mainland.

Most of the political philosophers of the "Enlightenment" of the eighteenth century, especially those in France, were dubious about Christianity and impatient with historic tradition. They wanted a liberation from the past, and they imagined that "science" and "reason" and "progress" would speedily usher in a brand-new world order of human freedom and happiness. Yet actually they followed in the footsteps of Locke, and, without recognizing it, in the essentially Christian tradition. They lauded "natural law" and "natural rights" as a St. Thomas Aquinas had done; and they were so imbued with the Christian concept of the dignity of man as to endow him with a most extraordinary rationality and perfectibility. They pointed the road to the American and French Revolutions, twin gateways to the broadening liberty of the nineteenth century.

Our America has certainly been a very fertile field for growing a bumper crop of personal liberty. This has been the result, in part, of the originally virgin character of the land and the naturally individualistic life and labor of immigrant frontiersmen upon it. As William Penn said about our colonial ancestors, they thought "nothing taller than themselves but the trees." Each felt, and on occasion would boast, that "I am as good as you are, except a bit better."

But this attitude was not induced so much by the new physical environment of colonial Americans as by the

Christian heritage they brought with them from Europe. Most of them were zealously Christian, and, like their revolutionary fellow Puritans in England a century before, they were seeking in the American Revolution to conserve the traditional rights of free men against royal aggression. Such a people took to the "liberating" doctrines of a John Locke, an Edmund Burke, or a Thomas Paine—very different in detail as these were—as easily as ducks to water. Thomas Jefferson, though himself a skeptic about Christianity, only generalized a popular and basically Christian conviction when he wrote in the Declaration of Independence that "all men are endowed by their Creator with certain unalienable rights," among which are "life, liberty, and the pursuit of happiness."

The same philosophy that dictated the Declaration of Independence was fundamental to the several state constitutions adopted between 1776 and 1780. The prime object was to itemize and secure those "unalienable rights," and each constitution contained a list of specific personal liberties. Most of these, moreover, were given added emphasis and application by their inclusion in the amendments of 1791 to the United States Constitution— our Federal Bill of Rights.

The outcome of the American Revolution, with its successful assertion of the principle of national self-determination and its elaboration of the principles of popular sovereignty and individual liberty, has had incalculable influence throughout the whole area of Western civilization. Its repercussion was immediate in France, where the famous "Declaration of the Rights of Man and of the

Citizen" was promulgated in 1789. "All men," it repeated, "are born and remain free and equal in rights," and these rights are "liberty, property, security, and resistance to oppression."

The ensuing years of the nineteenth century and the first two decades of our own century constituted a notable period of progressive human liberty. Not only did it witness a steady extension of the right of the individual to exercise political suffrage and thereby to have a say in the choice and actions of his government. It also witnessed an end of Negro slavery, a removal of restrictions on trade and on the right of association, whether of businessmen or of workers, and a concerted effort to raise the standard of living for everybody. "Liberty under law" became a commonly accepted dictum, and one nation after another proclaimed those individual liberties of religion, speech, press, assembly, petition, and justice which had been incorporated in the Constitution of the United States. It was indicative of the triumphant advance of liberty that when the present century began anyone could freely travel anywhere in America and in most of Europe without passport or police surveillance. "Iron curtains" were still in the future.

In sum, human freedom has been a pretty constant ideal and tradition of our Western civilization ever since this civilization was permeated by Christianity, and at least until our own day it has borne abundant fruit. Sometimes in practice, as I indicated earlier, it has been obscured or repressed by monarchs or oligarchies or by ecclesiastics whose external profession of Christianity has been in scandalous contrast with their selfish ambition and tyrannical mindedness. No doubt, too, many crimes have been committed down through the centuries in the name of liberty or under its guise. Sometimes a misapplied liberty has led to flagrant abuse, like the "economic liberty," with its "freedom of contract," which a hundred years ago was expounded by economists and espoused by professedly Christian industrialists.

We should constantly bear in mind that any religion, Christianity included, has to function among human beings, and that among these the lust for power and prestige and wealth is by no means uncommon or unusual. The wonder is not that there have been despotic rulers and eras in the long history of Western civilization. Rather, the wonder is that they have repeatedly given way to a rebirth of liberty. For to me, as an historian, it appears obvious that the Christian tradition of freedom has been so persistent and effective that up to now every actual setback to personal liberty has been followed, sooner or later, by a fresh advance.

3

Alas, in our century, new tyrants of peculiarly menacing character have arisen within, as well as outside, the Western world. They are new Genghiz Khans; and on an ever-broadening front they have mercilessly assailed the whole ideal of human freedom and have trampled down its every exercise. Two of them, the wild Hitler and the histrionic Mussolini, after causing terrible havoc within the free West, have met ignominious defeat and death. But the half-Oriental and half-barbarian masters of the Kremlin remain very much alive and continue to crush liberty throughout a domain that now stretches, far vaster than the original Genghiz Khan's, from the China Seas across all Asia and half of Europe to the Adriatic and the Elbe. And their despotism not only intrudes deeply into traditionally Western Christendom, covering with its terrors Hungary, Poland, Czechoslovakia, and half of Germany. What is still worse, it commands the outright allegiance, or apologetic sympathy, of sizable minorities in every country of the West.

There is no essential difference between the imperial bolshevism of the Kremlin and the national socialism of Hitler's type. Both are utterly unscrupulous. Both are quite antithetical to Christian faith and morality. Both are bitter foes of all political, religious, and civil liberty. Both regard the individual citizen as possessing no rights which can be asserted against the state and its dictatorship. Both trumpet the word "socialism" for demagogic reasons, but both begin by abolishing the right to strike and conclude by turning their workers into slave labor. The ruling class in both is an oligarchy of bureaucrats and police, whose chief attention is devoted to liquidating domestic dissent and to insulating their enslaved subjects against any liberal idea from abroad and employing them to pile up armaments. They are thoroughly reactionary movements, and their contemporary vogue represents an ominous break with the progress of past ages toward the attainment of human freedom.

But the startling setback to liberty in our generation

is attributable only in part to the strength and determination of its acknowledged foes. It is also attributable to a weakening of devotion and effort on the part of its traditional friends. How this has come about, I shall not here attempt to explain in any detail.*

I would remind you, however, that our American coins still emblazon the word "Liberty," and along with it the legend "In God We Trust," and that as yet the Supreme Court has not ruled the juxtaposition a violation of our constitutional principle of the separation of church and state. It does suggest that in our consideration of individuality and liberty, we have come full circle. For I began by pointing out the long and close connection between the liberty we have striven for in our Western civilization and the Judaeo-Graeco-Christian faith by which our ancestors were inspired.

Personally, I must confess a conviction, derived not only from faith but from historical study, that wherever Christian ideals have been generally accepted and their practice sincerely attempted, there is a dynamic liberty; and that wherever Christianity has been ignored or rejected, persecuted or chained to the state, there is tyranny. I, for one, am sure that our liberty and its Christian basis are indeed inseparable. This was significantly recognized by Hitler and has been systematically acted upon by the Communist regime in the Kremlin and its satraps abroad.

* I have suggested some explanations in two articles: "The Novelty of Totalitarianism in the History of Western Civilization," *Proceedings of the American Philosophical Society*, LXXXII (1940), 1–12; and "Liberty Revisited," *New York History*, XXXI (1950), 3–14.

They are surer of enslaving a nation if they gag or imprison clergymen, close churches, and de-Christianize the youth.

Liberty, in its Christian context, has always been a stimulant to independent thinking and an antidote to collective apathy. How very much now, when new tyrants apply opiates to the masses and do their thinking for them, do we need a rebirth of freedom. And I have such deep-seated faith in the Christian doctrine of the nature and dignity of man as to believe that in the long run, if he remains true to our Western traditions, he will rise again in revolt and free himself from the despotisms of the present age. Human freedom in any of its aspects can be maintained and forwarded, let us all remember, only through earnest and tireless effort of individuals.

There is another and closely related phase—or bulwark—of historic Western freedom, one which I shall discuss in the next chapter under the title of "Plural Authority and Constitutional Government." I conclude the present remarks on "Individuality and Liberty" by quoting in full the verse in the Epistle of St. James to which I have already alluded: "One who gazes into that perfect law, which is the law of freedom, and dwells on the sight of it, does not forget its message; he finds something to do, and he does it, and his doing of it wins him a blessing."

II. *Plural Authority and Constitutional Government*

WITHOUT authority, as has often been pointed out, liberty can become license, and society drift into chaos and anarchy. Particularly in the Christian West, where opposition to despotic authority has been so chronic, there has been a tendency on the part of some extremists to turn anarchist and to let each individual be his own and sole authority. (That was the case, for example, with early Christian hermits of the Egyptian and Syrian deserts, with so-called "spiritual" Franciscans of the fourteenth century, with certain radical Protestant sects of the sixteenth century, and with a number of nineteenth-century intellectuals in Russia, such as Bakunin, Kropotkin, and Tolstoy. Today, anarchism has its main popular following among peasants and workmen in traditionally Christian Latin Europe, especially in Spain. It is not without interest that it was Spanish Anarchists, more than Communists, who, under the late Spanish Republic, employed violence against the civil government, and killed or tortured bishops, priests, and nuns. The almost incredible story is told of many of those Anarchists that, on entering churches to desecrate them, they piously crossed themselves; the story would be quite incredible if one overlooked the relationship of their anarchism to a perverted concept of Christian liberty.

Personal liberty, in the age-long Christian tradition, has been coupled with, and qualified by, respect for authority. This was affirmed by Christ himself in the famous dictum, "Give to Caesar what is Caesar's, and to God what is God's." And it was reaffirmed by St. Peter in the oft-quoted words: "You are free men, but the liberty you enjoy is not to be made a pretext for wrong-doing; it is to be used in God's service. Give all men their due; to the brethren your love, to God your reverence, to the king due honor."

The most noteworthy feature about these counsels is that the authority they sanctioned was not unitary, but plural. Authority of Caesar or the king, that is, authority of the state, was recognized but it was not the only authority for Christian people. There was also the authority of God, exercised through the individual conscience and through the Apostles and their successors in the Christian church.

Here was the basis for restrictions on that omnipotence of the state which historically has characterized most civilizations other than our own. In the ancient pagan Roman Empire, for example, there was no distinction between the ruler's secular and religious authority; he was *pontifex maximus* as well as *imperator*, and his will in both spheres was paramount and decisive. It was similar with Mohammed and the succeeding caliphs of the Moslem world; only recently has there been some change in this respect in the Near and Middle East and then it has been imitative of the West rather than inherent in Islam. In Japan and China, too, where traditionally the emperors were regarded as deities or "sons of heaven," authority was essentially unitary.

In the West, on the contrary, a different tradition was implanted by the seed of Christian precept and practice. Christians of the first three centuries, while giving to the pagan Caesar what they thought was due him, felt an obligation to give to God what they believed was His, even if it meant defiance of Emperor and the penalty of death for themselves. They were willing to pay imperial taxes, to serve in the imperial army, and to obey imperial law in so far as this did not violate their Christian conscience and God's law. In other words, they had a divided allegiance; and on occasion, as is well known, they stubbornly refused to accord supreme authority to the state. They would not pay the Emperor the divine worship they reserved for God—not even would they burn a symbolic pinch of incense in the Emperor's honor.

The Apostles Peter and Paul, both of whom had preached obedience to civil authority, met a like fate at Rome for preaching another obedience to a higher authority. We have no record of their last days, but we do have a fairly detailed contemporaneous account of the martyrdom, and of what led up to it, of Ignatius, the saintly first-century Bishop of Antioch. It poignantly reveals not only the calmness and resignation with which the old man met death rather than deny Christ, but also the eloquence and persistence with which he begged his fellow Christians to stand firm in their faith. And many a Christian did stand firm, to the point of martyrdom, during the ensuing two centuries of spasmodic imperial persecution. They were witnesses to their faith, and likewise to the Christian doctrine of plural authority.

This doctrine received clear and repeated exemplification during the centuries when Christians constituted a minority in a pagan civilization and were charged with disloyalty to the pagan emperors. But it received further, and perhaps more startling, exemplification in the fourth century, when the conflict between paganism and Christianity for subsequent pre-eminence in Western civilization was largely decided in favor of the latter, and when Roman Emperors themselves turned from championship of paganism to that of Christianity. One might expect that newly professed Christian Emperors would claim the same sort of supreme authority, both religious and secular, as their pagan predecessors had exercised, and that a grateful Christian people might accord to Christian Emperors what they had refused to pagan. Constantine, the first Emperor to profess Christianity, frequently acted as if he was head of both church and state, and so, too, did some of his successors. Nevertheless, by the fourth century the doctrine of plural authority was so much a part of Western Christian tradition and teaching that it could not be successfully ignored or subverted by Emperors friendly to Christianity any more than by those inimical to it.

The Christian Emperor Gratian in the year 382 did away with the title of *pontifex maximus* which previous Emperors had borne, thus officially secularizing the state, so to speak, and disclaiming imperial authority in religious matters. Shortly afterward, in the year 390, the Christian Emperor Theodosius was publicly upbraided by an ecclesiastic, one of his subjects, the celebrated Bishop Ambrose of Milan, for having violated Christian ethics by an indiscriminate massacre of Thessalonians, and was summoned to do penance for his sin. At first the Emperor refused, and threatened Ambrose, but eventually his conscience as a Christian overcame his sense of authority as Emperor and he submitted to religious authority. The outcome is dramatically told by Ambrose: "Theodosius, stripping himself of every emblem of royalty, publicly in church bewailed his sin. Public penance, which private individuals shrink from, an Emperor was not ashamed to perform, nor was there afterwards a day on which he did not grieve for his wrongdoing." Ambrose pithily summed up the matter: "The Emperor is within the Church but not above the Church."

Roughly a century after Ambrose, the principle for which he stood was solemnly endorsed by Pope Gelasius I in the memorable pronouncement: "There are two powers by which chiefly this world is ruled—the sacred authority of the priesthood and the authority of kings. And of these the authority of the priests is so much the weightier as they must render before the tribunal of God an account even for the kings of men."

2

The latter part of this papal pronouncement of the fifth century—the part about the "weightier" authority of the clergy—was carried by medieval popes, notably by

Innocent III and Boniface VIII, to lengths which most modern Christians regard as dangerously excessive, and which aroused no little opposition among medieval Christians. About the authoritarian claims of medieval popes, several things should be borne in mind by modern critics. One is the fact that Christ himself, for whom those popes professed to speak, had only implied, and not detailed, just what is Caesar's and just what is God's; they felt called upon to supply particulars. Second is the fact that the circumstances and needs of their age were different from ours, and that their directions about church-state relationship, however applicable to their age, are not necessarily applicable to ours; in this respect, as in others, one should not judge the past by the present or the present by the past. Third is the fact that no immutable dogmatic character has been attributed, even by Catholics, to all the temporal claims of medieval popes.

There is a fourth fact, more significant than all the others, for a true understanding of the matter. It is this, that no medieval pope, whatever temporal authority he may have claimed or however strenuously he may have attempted to exercise it, ever denied the existence of authority other than his own. All medieval popes, to say nothing of ancient and modern, were mindful of Christ's instruction that there is an authority of Caesar's and the state's as well as of God's; that, in other words, there is a plural authority with a corresponding division of power.

Consequently, even at the period in our Western civilization when their power was greatest and widest, neither pope nor church exercised or aspired to any such theocracy as arose among Moslems or in Japan. On the contrary, pope and church, while insisting on their spiritual authority, constantly upheld the temporal and secular authority of the state. It was with papal encouragement that newly Christianized German and Slavic peoples were taught allegiance to their several kings and kingdoms. It was under papal auspices that a Christian Roman Empire was revived in the West, first under Charlemagne, and then under Otto. It was with papal blessing, and with the counsel of Christian prelates, that national monarchies developed in England, in Scandinavia, in Spain, and in France. Nor was there any question by pope, or church, of the right to the exercise of secular authority by republican governments in the Swiss cantons or in the city-states of Italy and Germany. Form of government was of minor importance; the major consideration was whether it limited its authority to its own sphere and did not infringe on the rights of spiritual authority.

Strictly speaking, *union* of church and state has never existed in our Western civilization. Co-operation, yes; but union, that is identity or amalgamation, no. This is attested and copiously illustrated by medieval as well as by modern history. There have been many disputes and conflicts between church and state, between ecclesiastics and secular rulers, over their respective "rights" and jurisdictions, but at least during the Middle Ages each side conceded to the other a considerable degree of independent authority. A stern pope like Gregory VII might challenge the claim of Emperor Henry IV to dominate the German bishops and he might succeed in humbling the Emperor by compelling him to retract and to do penance at Canossa barefoot amid snow and ice, but Gregory did not seek the destruction of the Empire nor the impairment of what he regarded as the Emperor's legitimate authority. On the other hand, ambitious monarchs like Henry II of England and Philip the Fair of France might challenge ecclesiastical claims in matters of taxation, appointments, and administration of justice, and in the ensuing struggles a Henry might bring to an archbishop death in his cathedral, or a Philip might employ such violence against a pope as to cause his death and to bring about the election of a more subservient pontiff. Yet neither Philip of France nor Henry of England, nor any other medieval Western monarch so far as I am aware, ever sought the abolition of papacy or church or denied it the exercise of what they regarded as its legitimate authority.

In fact, the idea of plural authority and division of power had become so widely accepted and seemed so natural throughout the West during the Middle Ages that popular support could usually be enlisted against undue or exaggerated claims of either churchmen or statesmen and conflicts between them, however bitter at the moment, normally ended in compromise. Only the content of what was Caesar's and what was God's fluctuated; the principle of a difference between them remained constant. And this principle undoubtedly was a bulwark of freedom for individuals and also for nations. It operated to check despotic rule and to fashion constitutional government.

3

For constitutional government, as we know and cherish it, is a heritage from the Christian Western Europe of the Middle Ages. Among the factors which then promoted it were two of basic importance and peculiarly Christian nature. One was the individuality—the sense of personal dignity, the aspiration to personal freedom—which, as I indicated in the previous chapter, was such a vital part of the preaching of Christ and his foremost Apostles. It was this which contributed immeasurably to the medieval popularity of the doctrine of natural rights and to its expression in the medieval charters of liberty that were wrested from monarchs in practically every country of the West. And Magna Carta and similar charters on the European continent not only served to protect groups and individuals of the time against arbitrary government; they were starting point and inspiration for the modern practice of incorporating **bills of rights** in instruments of constitutional government. Without them, it is hardly conceivable that the British should have produced the Bill of Rights of 1689 and preserved it as an integral part of their present constitution, or that the French in 1789 should have begun their modern revolutionary movement and constitutional experimentation with a Declaration of the Rights of Man and of the Citizen, or that the first amendments to our own American Federal Constitution—those of 1791—should have comprised a ten-articled bill of rights. The individual American, by merely mentioning the Fifth Amendment, may effectually block a governmental inquisition, which is something that cannot be done in anti-Christian Communist Russia, but which is curiously reminiscent of the medieval "benefit of clergy."

The second factor of peculiarly Christian nature in the rise of Western constitutional government was the concept of plural authority of which I am here treating. The concept was primarily, as we have seen, of a division and separation of power between state and church, between temporal and spiritual authority. But it led, more or less naturally and logically, to the corollary that the state itself, in its own sphere, was not monolithic. Rather, it was conceived of as corporative, exercising its authority in large part through delegation of powers to entities and groups within it, such as clergy, nobility, provinces, towns, guilds, universities, etc. Such groups sought and frequently obtained charters that accorded them certain corporate rights, immunities, and privileges. As pressure groups, moreover, they exercised no little influence on state administration and policy; and, gradually, formal bodies, representative of them, were accorded some share in legislation. These bodies might be two-fold, as in the English Parliament, or three-fold, as in the French Estates-General, or four-fold, as in the Estates of Aragon or Sweden; and, depending on local circumstance, they might differ greatly in the scope and efficacy of their power. Yet everywhere throughout the West they embodied the principle of plural authority and inaugurated the tradition that constitutional government, in addition to guaranteeing personal liberties, should be representative government. They were forerunners in a sense, too, of the provision in our American Constitution for "checks and balances" and "separation of powers."

4

To maintain in practice the principles of plural authority and constitutional government which emanated from Christian teaching and found special expression in Western Europe in the Middle Ages has always proved difficult. The Middle Ages themselves furnished no exception to this generalization, and toward their close, in the era of the Renaissance, a variety of circumstances—economic, political, military, ecclesiastical, and intellectual—combined to exalt royal authority as it had not been exalted since much earlier times.

This development, like the Renaissance itself, was reactionary in essence. It involved a departure from political as well as other lines of medieval Christian development and a return to pagan antiquity for models of statecraft no less than of architecture and art. It was exemplified, I need hardly remind you, by the crop of Italian despots who flourished in the fifteenth and sixteenth centuries, and by a contemporaneous galaxy of national monarchs in England, France, Spain, and Scandinavia; and its philosophy was unblushingly expounded in Machiavelli's *The Prince*. And popes of the time, while formally condemning the teaching of Machiavelli, actually embraced it, and they and many other prelates showed greater concern with temporal than with spiritual affairs.

Nevertheless, Christian conscience and tradition were too deeply imbedded in the West to admit of eradication in the sixteenth century. On the contrary, they reasserted themselves in the religious upheaval of that century—alike in Protestant revolt and in Catholic reformation. If Catholicism reaffirmed the traditional faith, new-born Protestantism re-emphasized individuality and the role of conscience. If the one continued to insist upon the authority of the church, the other, in repudiating that authority, still championed, in the Bible, the "written Word of God," an authority beyond that of the state.

The conflict which raged in the sixteenth and into the seventeenth centuries between Protestants and Catholics was far from edifying. It was attended, we all know, by a fanaticism and an intolerance, by persecution and violence and slaughter, which have seldom been surpassed in European annals and which appear to us moderns as quite out of keeping with any conception of Christian charity. True, there was vast sincerity on both sides. Many a Catholic leader was convinced that he was defending Western civilization against anarchy and barbarism. Many a Protestant leader was equally convinced that he was purifying Western civilization of corruption and superstition.

Moreover, each side in the conflict, in order to defeat the other, usually invoked the power of the state and conceded to the state a control scarcely compatible with the traditional practice of plural authority. Martin Luther appealed to the German princes for support, advising them that they could better themselves materially, as well as spiritually, by repudiating papal authority and expropriating church property; and many German princes, along with sovereigns of Denmark, Sweden, and England, acted accordingly. At the same time, the papacy managed to retain at least the avowed loyalty of other sovereigns, notably those of Spain, Portugal, France, and Austria, by conceding to them a control of ecclesiastical appointments, courts, and finance which severely restricted church authority while increasing that of the state. Altogether, the religious upheaval of the sixteenth century served to speed the rise of that type of absolutist divine-right monarchy which reached its height under the Stuart kings of the seventeenth century in Britain, and the Bourbon, Habsburg, Hohenzollern, and other Continental monarchs of the eighteenth century. In every country, there was a state church and, whether Protestant or Catholic, it seemed but a dependency or department of secular government.

Christian leaven remained, however; and it "worked," and helped eventually to produce violent reaction against political absolutism. Among Protestants, followers of John Calvin were particularly conspicuous in their stand against monarchical despotism and for church independence, and so too were Puritan Anglicans and such radical sects as Congregationalists, Baptists, Quakers, etc. Without their Christian convictions and their militancy in asserting them, it is inconceivable to me that England would have pursued the revolutionary course it did in the seventeenth century and re-established constitutional government on a firm basis, with limitations on its exercise and with guarantees of religious freedom for Christian dissenters from the state church. Nor is it conceivable to me that without similar Protestant Christian conviction and militancy the American Revolution would have occurred or would soon have been followed by our Federal Constitution and its first ten amendments, in which again the principle of plural authority is affirmed, most significantly perhaps, in the very first amendment: "Congress shall make no laws respecting an establishment of religion, or prohibiting the free exercise thereof." In the United States there may be co-operation between state and church, but definitely no union.

Simultaneously, among Catholics, there were outstanding and outspoken opponents of royal despotism and its abridgment not only of traditional "rights" of the church, but also of "natural rights" common to all men. I here have in mind such persons as Cardinal Bellarmine in Italy and the Jesuit Suárez in Spain. We may likewise recall that both aristocratic Catholic Poland and the democratic Catholic cantons of Switzerland stoutly resisted any imposition of despotic government. And it is not without interest that the great French Revolution of 1789, with its Declaration of the Rights of Man and its epochal overthrow of royal absolutism, was led for the most part by persons who, though professing an "enlightened" skepticism about Christianity, had been educated in Catholic schools. In our own country, we may recall, the first Catholic bishop, John Carroll, was an outstanding patriot and liberal, and his kinsman, Charles Carroll of Carrollton, was a signer, along with Thomas Jefferson, of the Declaration of Independence.

5

From the time of the American and French Revolutions down to the present day, Western civilization has been more and more secularized. The state has steadily extended its activities and gradually taken over one after another function formerly discharged by the church: education of youth; care of the sick, the poor, the aged, the unfortunate generally; concern with such personal and family matters as birth, marriage, divorce, death, and inheritance. Nowadays, every American citizen, if he likes, can be quite free of any religious observance, but, whether he likes it or not, he must pay taxes for the support of state schools, he must contribute to a variety of state funds for social welfare, his birth must be registered by the state, he must obtain from the state a license to marry, and when he dies he is likely to be embalmed and laid out in a funeral home or mortuary parlor authorized and inspected by the state, and, of course, the state insists on having a record of his demise and a share of his inheritance.

This secularization — this enlargement of state functions—is by no means peculiar to the United States, or to the kindred countries of western and central Europe. It has latterly spread outside the traditionally Christian areas of the world and has well nigh revolutionized the relationship between religion and secular government in Moslem Turkey and Iran, in Buddhist Japan and China, in Hindu India. To it, several modern developments have contributed.

One is nationalism, the idea that the national state, as contrasted with an imperial, feudal, or city state, incorporates and can best serve the common interests of a particular people or nationality. There is no doubt about the popularity of nationalism in the contemporary world, or about the role the national state plays or is expected to play in subordinating other loyalties of its citizens to a superior loyalty to itself.

Because nationalism, as we know it, had its origin in Western Europe and was there first embodied in national states, some Christian apologists, especially among romantics of a century ago, have argued that it is basically Christian, a natural application of the Christian principle of individuality to national and international life. There may be an element of truth in the argument if we consider the relatively early and specifically humanitarian nationalism advocated by the German Herder, the French Chateaubriand, or the Italian Mazzini. But in its development nationalism has often turned out to be the handmaid of secularism, and, as recently exemplified by Mussolini and Hitler, a complete perversion of Christianity.

Another and more obvious development contributing to the enlargement of state functions has been the modern revolution in technology, industry, and communications. For this revolution has made our present ways of living, working, and traveling very different from our ancestors' ways. It has transformed society and affected every individual throughout Christendom—and beyond. Besides, it has created a situation deleterious to historic tradition and favorable to novel experiments in politics and economics.

Consider, for instance, the effect of the industrial revolution on the masses of a nation. Previously, the bulk of these had engaged in farming and had been relatively settled in body and mind. Now they are migratory, nomadic, almost gypsy-like. They move from country to town, from town to city, from one house to another. This means that they have become what the French call *déracinés*, that is, uprooted from ancestral soil, from established habit and tradition. They may make more money than their fathers made, but they do so in an atmosphere and chronic dread of economic insecurity. Hence, to safeguard themselves, they more or less naturally turn to collectivism—to trade-unionism or socialism—and demand state intervention in their behalf. And the contemporary national democratic state is likely to be responsive to such demands. We Americans are now quite used to "new deals" and "fair deals," and we should expect no retreat from them by any Democratic—or Republican—administration. It is, indeed, in the big new industrial field that secular government is expanding its functions most widely and most surely.

In calling attention to the big increase of state functions and authority in our contemporary age of nationalism and machine industry, I do not mean to imply that I am hostile to, or unsympathetic with, the central purpose of the new trend. Quite the contrary! There is real need, in my opinion, of adapting our institutions and practices to a new and radically changed social and economic environment, and while I earnestly hope that traditional religious values and counsels will not be sacrificed or overlooked in the process, I fully recognize that secular authority must be the actual agency of social reform.

6

The most disturbing attendant of modern industrialization is an exaggerated materialism, an absorption in material things to the exclusion or neglect of the spiritual. It has possessed so-called "captains of industry"—business promoters and executives, bankers and brokers, tradesmen and traveling salesmen. It has also possessed workmen in factory, foundry, and mine, in shop and office. Its popularity in America is attested by the widespread assumption that we can *buy* friends and allies abroad. Probably most of us are materialistic rather blindly and unconsciously, but not so the apostles of Marxian communism and their fast-growing number of disciplined disciples throughout the world. Their materialism admits of no plural authority, no divided allegiance.

Karl Marx himself was a product of Western civilization, and he was undoubtedly motivated in part by some of its fundamental spiritual ideals, notably by compassion for exploited fellow men and by hope in the coming of a kind of kingdom of God on earth. But Marx's philosophy, his interpretation of history, and the practical measures he urged for attaining his proletarian paradise were all strictly materialistic. Together they represent a complete perversion of the historic ideals of Western civilization, or, as Arnold Toynbee calls it, a supreme Christian heresy.

The West did not take immediately to Marxism. Not until 1917 was it translated into action, and then, what would have astounded Marx, the revolution occurred in Russia. It was quite ironical. Marx had prophesied that only in an industrialized country, with a large urban proletariat, could a Communist revolution succeed; Russia was a largely agricultural country, with a comparatively small urban proletariat. Furthermore, Marx intensely disliked Russia and deemed it too barbarous, too bound by traditions of autocracy and serfdom, to be capable of ushering in the Communist paradise he envisaged.

In this latter judgment, Marx was unusually correct. Russia had never fully shared in the civilization of the West. Christianity entered it comparatively late and with a dependence on the monarch, a Caesaro-papism, which was borrowed from Byzantium and the East and had only fleeting influence in the West. Concepts of personal liberty, of plural authority and representative government, so persistent and so fruitful in the West, were alien to Russia; modern Russians who entertained them were rightly labeled "Westernizers" and popularly regarded as suspect. As in the ancient East, so in medieval and modern Russia, palace revolutions were fairly frequent, but they only replaced one autocratic ruler with another; autocracy continued.

The Communist revolution of 1917 has proved to be more in the nature of the traditional Russian palace revolution than of the "liberating" movement which Marx had hoped for. It replaced the autocratic Tsar Nicholas with a new and more plebeian line of autocrats from Lenin to the present Malenkov. Nor have there been any signs of that "withering away" of the state which Marx predicted. On the contrary, the Communist regime has sacrificed liberty to authority. And its authority, like Peter the Great's, is not plural; it is emphatically singular. Whether veiled as a "dictatorship of the proletariat" or as a "people's democratic republic," autocracy continues in Russia.

There are differences, of course, but they are mainly differences of degree and method. The Communist regime has been more efficient and more ruthless than the Tsardom; and, by concentrating on material objectives, it has fostered a much greater industrialization of the country, both rural and urban. This has been accomplished, however, by rendering Russia more of a police-state than ever before. Labor is more rigidly controlled, and more of it amounts to slave-labor. The Tsardom's suppression of dissent on the part of individuals or groups was spasmodic and partial; the Communist regime's is constant and rigorous, and apparently successful. Nowadays no Russian may say, or write, or do, or be suspected of thinking, anything that is not in accord with the "party line" laid down in the Kremlin; if he does, the police are pretty sure to get him, and he'd better confess and be prepared for "liquidation."

The Communist regime maintains far more effective armed forces than did the Tsardom, and, with their aid, it has been much more successful in imperialistic enterprise. Russian Panslavism, once a mere dream, is now a stark reality, except, possibly, in the case of Yugoslavia. Russian imperialism in the Far East, interrupted in the time of Tsar Nicholas II, has been resumed by the present dictatorship on a vaster scale, with the huge domain of China and half of Korea already subjected to Communist rulers dependent upon the Kremlin. Knowing that China and Korea, like Russia itself, are outside the area of our historic Western civilization, we might reasonably infer that they would fall victim more easily than Western nations to Communist dictatorship, with its denial of individual liberty and any divided authority. But *inside* the area of Western civilization, Russian imperialistic communism has likewise engulfed six nations, and parts of two others, each of which is now a satellite of the Kremlin, faithfully reflecting its monolithic structure and its tyranny.

It is to be noted that none of the nations which have turned from Western ideals of freedom to Communist practice of tyranny have done so of their own free will and accord. They have been driven into captivity by occupying or threatening Russian armies, with, unfortunately, the connivance and co-operation of a minority of self-seeking Marxist natives. These latter, once in power, have retained it by using the same methods as those employed by their mentors and props in Communist Russia.

It is not reassuring that in other nations, such as France and Italy, geographically more remote from Communist Russia, and longer and more closely identified with the West, there are now very sizable minorities of avowed Communists, apparently willing to exchange their Western spiritual inheritance for a mess of Russian pottage. That Communist Russia does not forcibly extend its despotic imperialism over the whole Atlantic Community of our Western civilization can only be attributed to its fear of the community's material and armed strength, and particularly of America's. But our strength, and let me emphasize this, is not purely material or strictly military. It lies fundamentally in our *will* to preserve our way of life and our heritage of liberty.

Our heritage of liberty, let me also emphasize, is buttressed by our heritage of plural authority. We cannot vest complete and sole authority in the secular state without rendering it ultimately despotic in the Russian Communist manner. Amid ever-increasing functions which the present industrial age practically requires the state to exercise, we must contrive to respect and to safeguard some of the traditional authority of the individual, of the family, and of the churches, especially in the fields of education and ethics. Above all, it is still needful, I submit, to give not only "to Caesar what is Caesar's" but "to God what is God's."

III. *Progress and Compassion*

1

AMONG the features of our Western civilization which have been influenced and in large part shaped by its historic religious doctrines and beliefs, I have already discussed two. One is the peculiarly Christian emphasis on individuality and liberty, on the dignity of the person, which has made for "liberty, equality, and fraternity" and pointed the way toward social and political democracy. A second is the Christian respect for authority as a safeguard against anarchy, but for a *plural* authority, a division of powers between God and the state and also within the state. This has been a safeguard against despotism and a prime contributor to making the West the home of constitutional government with its guarantees of personal freedom. To a third feature I now invite attention. It is the progressive, dynamic character of Western civilization, particularly in regard to developing and expanding application of the Christian ideal of compassion.

I suppose there is no word that enjoys greater popularity today in the United States than the word "progressive." Who among us would like to be called or thought of as "unprogressive"? Who among us, imbued with the idea of progress, does not strive to be "forward-looking," whether or not he ever looks backward into history?

If he were backward-looking, he would find, I think, ample justification in history for his contemporary belief in progress. For our Western civilization has not tended to become static or stereotyped, as have certain other civilizations.

It has been claimed by some historical scholars, most notably perhaps by the late Professor Bury of Cambridge, that our idea of progress is not very old; that it did not emerge until the Enlightenment of the eighteenth century. Possibly this is true. It is curious, however, that the Enlightenment and its idea of progress arose and flourished in a traditionally Christian, not Moslem or Buddhist or Hindu, environment. And no matter when the *idea* became prevalent, the *fact* of progress has long been an observable feature of the Western world.

Indeed, the dynamic character of our Western civilization curiously parallels the dynamic character of the Christian religion. This may be merely coincidental, but I do not think so. Christianity has been an especially outgoing and zealously proselyting religion. To be sure, it has not been the only missionary and proselyting world religion. Buddhism, originating in India, spread through the Far East; and Islam's extension was even farther, from Arabia through the Near and Middle East, over the northern half of Africa and over all Indonesia. Yet, social and intellectual developments in the East, where Buddhism and Islam are the traditionally dominant religions, have been less progressive than in the traditionally Christian West. If, in the present age, the East exhibits an unwonted progress, is it not attributable, in great part, to Western

influence, especially to the influence of Christian missionaries and Christian ideas? For after all, neither Moslem
nor Buddhist missionaries have penetrated Europe and
America in such numbers or with such effect as have Christian missionaries penetrated Asia.

It is frequently claimed, particularly by persons inclined to accept an economic interpretation of history, that
the differences and contrasts between East and West are
explicable in economic terms. I, for one, doubt it. The
potential wealth and natural resources of Asia have long
been greater than those of Europe, and the East could have
developed and exploited them earlier and in superior
fashion if it had had the West's dynamism. It is true, of
course, that the relative poverty of Europe and its desire
for profitable procurement of luxuries from the East served
as special stimuli for European traders and businessmen to
accompany and follow Christian missionaries into India
and the Far East and subsequently into Africa, and for
European governments to patronize and encourage in
modern times an amazing amount of Western imperialism,
economic and political. It is also true that this process has
been attended by an exploitation of native peoples and a
ruthlessness on the part of the West quite out of keeping
with its professed religion and quite embarrassing to Christian missionaries.

We should not forget, however, that in the long annals
of history, recurrent waves of Eastern imperialism have
beaten against the West. There were the Hunnish inva-
sions of the fifth century, the Moslem conquest of the
Iberian peninsula in the eighth century, and of the Balkans

and most of Hungary in the fifteenth and sixteenth centuries, with the culminating Moslem siege of Vienna in the seventeenth century. There was likewise the super-imperialism of Genghiz Khan and his Mongol hordes in the thirteenth century; and today we are faced with an Oriental axis of Communist imperialism with twin centers at Moscow and Peking.

Nor should we forget that, at least until now, while the West has had sufficient impulse and force to resist and overcome each wave of Eastern imperialism, the East, lacking that impulse and force, has more or less supinely submitted to imperialism, not only of the West, but more usually of its own creation. Even now the nationalism which is inspiring the East to get rid of Western imperialism is something, along with technology, which the East has learned from the West; and it is a big question of today and tomorrow whether in the East the newly acquired nationalism will not be supplanted by a new Eastern imperialism, that of Russian communism. At any rate, we Americans, as heirs of Western civilization, seem to have the impulse and will, which West Europeans of past centuries have had, to defend it against the latest imperial threat from the East.

2

There can be no doubt about the progress which the West has made down through the centuries, and particularly through modern times, in metallurgy and technology, in industry and agriculture, in commerce and communication. I do not propose to discuss this kind of progress here, principally because, as I have already said, the material aspects of our civilization can be, and have been, easily borrowed by and superimposed on other civilizations. Nowadays, technological advance is no monopoly or peculiarity of the West.

Rather, the progress which I have in mind as peculiar to the West, and which I venture to outline here, is not in the economic or material sphere. It is more basic. It has to do with spiritual progress along lines indicated by St. Paul in his first epistle to the Corinthians: "Make charity your aim, the spiritual gifts your aspiration."

Paul was but echoing the words and commemorating the example of his Master. Christ's Gospel had been addressed to individuals and was fundamentally concerned with individual salvation, but this could not be achieved if the individual was self-centered. He must be God-centered and must share with Christ, the God-Man, a love, a charity, for all other individuals. He must love his neighbor as himself. He must, like Christ, be filled with compassion; that is, he must suffer with his fellow men and bear with them their burdens.

As I reminded you earlier, Christ laid out no particular program of social reform or social betterment. But he did charge his individual disciples with a mission which had obvious social implications and obligations, and he left to them its progressive development and application. "I have still much to say to you," he told his apostles, "but it is beyond your reach as yet. It will be for the truth-giving Spirit, when he comes, to guide you into all truth." The progressive character of his gospel Christ emphasized on another occasion in another way: "Every scholar whose learning is of the kingdom of heaven," he said, "must be like a rich man who knows how to bring out of his treasure house new as well as old things." *New* as well as old! And the final test of Christians is pragmatic: "By their fruits you will know them."

Nineteen centuries have since elapsed, and they have borne witness in every generation to the sorry fact that profession of Christianity is no guarantee of Christian living and doing. The number of persons in our Western world who have taken to heart and observed Christ's precepts of love and compassion has probably been surpassed by those who have ignored or merely paid lip service to them. We must not blink this fact, or the further fact that many a non-Christian has exhibited, down through the ages, a compassion for his fellow men which should put many a professed Christian to shame.

Nevertheless, after making full allowance for the shortcomings of individual Christians, both clerical and lay, and for the natural sense of justice and mercy in humankind generally, we should recognize that the leaven of Christ's teaching has been potent and persistent enough to render our Western civilization more progressive than any other in humanitarian impulses and accomplishments. That so much lip service has been paid to the teaching is evidence in itself of the teaching's hold on the conscience of the West. With us, no skeptic or hypocrite or malefactor can quite forget it or entirely escape its influence.

Charity and compassion have been not only ideals of the Christian West; they have inspired so much of our thought, our laws, our attitudes, our actions. No sooner did the old Roman Empire pass from pagan to Christian leadership than the Emperors of the fourth century proceeded to promulgate laws against delation, defamation, usury, selling of young children, gladiatorial combats, and military excesses, and likewise against immodesty, adultery, and unnatural vices.

At first, slavery as an institution was not questioned. In pre-Christian times it had been so commonplace, so long and so much an established practice all over the world. Toward slaves, however, a new attitude was voiced by St. Paul in the delightful and appealing little letter which he addressed from Rome to a certain Philemon concerning one of the latter's slaves, by the name of Onesimus, who had run away to be with Paul and was now being sent back. "Do not think of him as a slave," wrote Paul; "he is something more than a slave, he is a well loved brother. . . . As thou dost value thy friendship with me, make him welcome as thou wouldst myself; if he has wronged thee, or is in thy debt, make me answerable for it."

By the fourth and fifth centuries, slavery itself was being reproved and reprobated by outstanding Christian writers, notably St. Gregory of Nyssa and St. John Chrysostom. And gradually throughout the Christianized areas of central and western Europe, slavery was moderated into serfdom and this, in time, gave way to freedom. The process of emancipation, characteristic of the West, may have been influenced by economic motives, but the principal cause, as I see it, was Christianity, acting through the authority of its teaching and the influence of its charity.

Though European slavery had long since disappeared, the discovery and settlement of the American continents were followed here, we all know, by a recrudescence of slavery, first of native Indians and then of imported African Negroes. But here again the Christian conscience revolted and gradually wrought a change. The pleas of a Spanish Catholic priest, Bartolomé de Las Casas, were chiefly responsible for emancipating the Indians; and in the forefront of the movement for emancipating the Negroes were the Anglican William Wilberforce, the Quakers, the French Society of Friends of the Blacks with its Catholic setting, and the New England Abolitionists with their Puritan background. The slave trade with Africa, so far as Great Britain was concerned, was abolished in 1807, and for the other European powers it was condemned by the Congress of Vienna in 1815. Although the abolition of Negro slavery in the United States was accomplished only after a terrible civil war, it was achieved peacefully in Brazil and Spanish America and throughout the British Empire. In still more recent times, the campaign against slavery has been carried by Christian missionaries and traditionally Christian nations into Africa itself. Only in Communist Russia, outside the historic area of Western civilization, is there now a reaction toward slave labor.

A religion whose Founder grew up in a carpentry shop, and most of whose first Apostles were fishermen, could hardly dissociate the dignity of manual labor from the dignity of man. From the time when St. Paul commended the slave Onesimus as a well-loved brother, no Christian theologian, so far as I am aware, has ever deemed workingmen spiritually inferior to anybody else or belittled their labor. Indeed, a common taunt of ancient pagans against Christianity was that it was a religion of the common people, of artisans and servants, a taunt which is sometimes echoed nowadays by snobs and pseudo-intellectuals. Certainly the medieval Western masses—peasants and handicraftsmen or guildsmen—worked long and hard, with few of the comforts which are now available to their descendants. But they took pride in their work, and were respected and honored for it. They possessed rights as well as duties. In general, they were much better off than corresponding classes outside the West.

Some pretty bad labor conditions attended the modern transition of the West from a predominantly agricultural to a predominantly industrial economy and society. It was these conditions which evoked the wrath of Karl Marx and provided the impetus for the rise of Marxian socialism. But these conditions also shocked the conscience of many a Christian, and aroused some of them to action before Marx had been heard of. And the remedying of bad labor conditions has continued to be urged by innumerable churchmen, including Shaftesbury, Kingsley, Cardinal Manning, and Bishop Gore in England, Ozanam and De Mun and Cardinal Suhard in France, Bishop von Ketteler and Friedrich Naumann in Germany, Popes Leo XIII and Pius XI, the Protestant Federal Council of Churches and the National Catholic Welfare Conference in the United States. Nor should we be unmindful of the co-operation in all this of religious Jews.

Religiously inspired people may have been less noisy

than atheistic Marxists about labor, but up to now, at any rate, it is the former who have done most to better labor conditions in the West. Without Christian influence and support, it is unthinkable to me that the pioneering Bismarckian labor legislation would have been enacted in Germany in the 1880's, or the Lloyd George legislation in Great Britain prior to the World War of 1914, or the more recent legislation of the New Deal and Fair Deal in the United States. Nations of the West are especially aware of the need and duty of raising the "standard of living" for the masses, and it is from the West that such need and duty are being impressed upon the East. While we in the United States boast of our "American way of life," we tax ourselves to furnish financial aid to spread it afar.

3

There has been a fairly constant and fruitful tradition in the Christian West that the individual is his brother's keeper, and that the more fortunate members of society owe something to the less fortunate, and the stronger to the weaker. This was exemplified by the knightly chivalry of the Middle Ages; and the later caricaturing of an extravagant and decadent chivalry, as in the *Don Quixote* of Cervantes, could not have enjoyed an immense popularity except in a civilization in which real chivalry has been a familiar phenomenon. For its principle of *noblesse oblige* has been as inspiring and operative in our democratic society of modern times as among medieval knights and nobles. And when we of the West encounter or hear about unchivalrous and uncharitable behavior among us, as we all too frequently do, we normally, in accordance with our heritage, experience a sense of shock and disgust.

I doubt whether women are really the weaker sex. But I am sure they have had greater opportunity to show their strength in our Western civilization than in any other. Christianity has always taught not only the spiritual equality of women with men but the duty of men to put women on a pedestal, to honor and revere them. In the West, there has never been any secluding of women in harems, or any burning of widows, not even of mothers-in-law. On the contrary, the history of the Christian West is replete with famous names of women saints, women sovereigns, women leaders in all walks of life—such names, for example, as Catherine of Siena and Teresa of Avila, the Elizabeths of England and Isabella of Castile, Countess Matilda and the Archduchess Maria Theresa, Jane Austen and Rosa Bonheur, Clara Barton and Marie Curie. Our women, too, are great managers, whether for medieval peasants or for modern business executives. They nowadays well nigh monopolize our typewriters and telephone centrals and the teaching in our schools; and before long, I suspect, men may be struggling for equal rights with women.

In behalf of children, likewise, the West has been particularly solicitous ever since it was impregnated by the Christian Gospel. Christ repeatedly held up children as models for the heavenly kingdom, and some of his bitterest words were directed against those who would abuse or scandalize children. Undoubtedly the most popular festival of the Western world is Christmas, the birthday of the Christ child. Not only has the Christian West had a special abhorrence of infanticide, tolerated and practiced else-where, but it has set an example to the rest of the world in child care, from orphanages to juvenile courts, societies and laws for the prevention of cruelty to children, organization of boy and girl scouts.

The preciousness of human life is reflected in the tra-ditional attitude of the West toward infanticide. It is also reflected in the West's abhorrence of suicide. To take one's own life has seemed even worse than to take an-other's. No honor has been associated with it, as has been the case, for example, in Japan or with an ancient pagan philosopher like Socrates. For long, Christian burial was denied to anybody who committed suicide, and latterly we charitably assume that such a one must be insane or else, like Hitler and other top Nazis, appropriately climaxing a most un-Christian career. Contemporary reaction against the mass racial murders of a Hitler is naturally and logi-cally expressed in the West's present campaign for inter-national condemnation and outlawing of genocide.

From the wellsprings of Christian compassion, our Western civilization has drawn its inspiration, and its sense of duty, for feeding the hungry, giving drink to the thirsty, looking after the homeless, clothing the naked, tending the sick, and visiting the prisoner. "Good works" have progressively abounded among us from those re-corded in the New Testament to our contemporary efforts to provide homes for displaced persons, to ship clothing and "Care" packages to war victims abroad, and to effect prison and housing reforms at home. If Christian mission-aries have not converted to their faith the masses of the

Far and Middle East, they have at least aroused in them a regard for Christian "good works."

Particularly noteworthy has been the Christian contribution to hospital development in the West. "Heal the sick," enjoined Christ; and so assiduously did the Christians of the first three centuries apply the injunction to hospital care of the sick that in the fourth century the apostate Emperor Julian urged his pagan followers, as the best means of circumventing the Christians, to emulate them in conducting hospitals. Julian failed; and quickly afterward, under the enthusiastic leadership of St. Basil of Caesarea, Christians were redoubling their efforts in behalf of the sick and infirm. Thenceforth there was a multiplication of hospitals—hospitals for the sick, for foundlings, for orphans, for the poor unable to work, for the aged, for poor or infirm pilgrims, for the insane.

In the Middle Ages, a special order, the Knights Hospitallers of St. John of Jerusalem, did a great work in caring for sick or wounded Crusaders, and after their expulsion from Jerusalem they continued their charitable support of hospitals from their headquarters, first at Rhodes, then at Malta, and now at Rome. Nor should we overlook the great work, in this field, of that seventeenth-century French saint, Vincent de Paul, or of the multitude of Sisters of Charity, including our American, Mother Elizabeth Seton, who are his spiritual daughters and have followed in his footsteps to the present day.

Of course, Protestants have shared with Catholics in care of the sick and in all the other Christian works of mercy. Every major Christian denomination maintains some sort of hospital—very many kinds in the case of Anglican, Lutheran, and Calvinist churches. There is the same inspiration back of the homes and refuges of the Salvation Army and the houses of hospitality of the Catholic Worker group.

Accompanying the very real progress which has been made down through the centuries in hospitals and general care of the sick and infirm, there has been a very notable and distinctive advance, in the West, of medical science and surgery. Indeed, our typical modern hospital represents compassionate solicitude for suffering, ennobled by Christian charity and made efficient by medical skill and science. Nowadays, many hospitals are maintained by state, city, or town, rather than by a church, but they too reflect and help to preserve the spirit of the West's traditional religion.

Where else than in the Christian West would one expect to find the origin and chief functioning of such an institution as the Red Cross? Where else, such vigorous campaigns against polio or cancer or heart disease? Where else, such things as "community chests" and "march of dimes"? Applied compassion, in all the respects I have mentioned, is essentially an enterprise and basically a mark of the Western world, of the Atlantic Community. In so far as it has penetrated and been imitated elsewhere, it has represented an export from the West, a fruit of the teaching and example of a Father Damien, a Dr. David Livingstone, and thousands upon thousands of other Christian-inspired missionaries. Historically, it has been taught to, but not by, the Far East, Africa, and Indian America. Its source is in the West.

4

Let me now briefly discuss another and more anomalous aspect of our Western civilization. I refer to pacifism and the problem of recurrent war. Some difficulty here, I think, arises from differences among us about Christ's teaching in the matter, and particularly about the translation of the famous angelic chorus in St. Luke's Gospel. The King James version has it: "Glory to God in the highest, and on earth peace, good will to men"; and this has sunk deeply into the minds and hearts of English-speaking people. There are grounds for doubting, however, whether it is an accurate translation. Preferable is the reading in the Douai version: "Glory to God in the highest, and on earth peace to men of good will," or in the recent version of Monsignor Knox: "Glory to God in high heaven, and peace on earth to men that are God's friends." These seem not only more accurate renderings of the original Greek but more in harmony with Christ's own utterances and attitude. "Do not imagine," he said, "that I have come to bring peace to the earth; I have come to bring a sword, not peace."

Christ apparently let his disciples carry swords, though when they asked him if they should use them to prevent his arrest his answer was no. "Let them [the officials] have their own way in this," he said. Christ certainly admired and praised a Roman army captain, and offered no criticism of his occupation. Moreover, many an early Christian served in Roman legions, and some notable ones among them, like Cornelius and Laurence, for instance, were honored as saints by their fellow Christians.

Christ did urge a striving for peace on the part of men of good will, on the part of "God's friends." "Peace be with you," was his reiterated greeting to his disciples, as it has been in church service books down through the ages. "Blessed are the peacemakers," declared Christ; "they should be counted the children of God."

Actually, peacemakers have always had to contend with warmakers within as well as outside the area of our Western civilization. For war and combativeness have been, everywhere and from time immemorial, so common, so recurrent, and so evidently natural to human beings as to admit of only partial, if any, control by spiritual, religious forces. Yet in our Western world, Christianity has implanted at least an ideal of peace, and has inspired a variety of efforts to check or minimize wars and to lessen their evils.

One such effort has been the distinction drawn by Western theologians and philosophers between the "just" and the "unjust" war, between defensive war and a war of aggression. In the "just" category, the Christian conscience was inclined to put the medieval crusades as being defensive wars against Moslem aggression, and likewise some of the religious wars of the sixteenth century, though here it depended upon whether the conscience was Protestant or Catholic: each imagined that by taking up arms it was defending itself against aggression by the other. Instead of peace, however, the inter-Christian fighting led to a series of dynastic and colonial wars which only a violent stretch of the imagination could consider "just." In our century, every Western nation, upon engaging in war, takes pains to declare that its cause is "just"—which at any rate is something of a verbal tribute to Christian tradition.

To check war and to lessen its ills, the medieval church instituted those interesting experiments known as the truce of God and the peace of God, and insisted upon the so-called right of asylum. Though the experiments themselves were not very successful, they indirectly contributed to the abatement and eventual extinction, under state authority, of feudal warfare. Besides, church condemnation has been an important factor in the modern decline and practical disappearance of dueling.

International war has continued, and in our century it has assumed terrifying proportions. Yet it is in the West and mainly under Christian inspiration that the most serious attempts have been made to promote international peace. There was the scheme of the French lawyer, Pierre Dubois, back in the fourteenth century. There was the development of international law by such pioneers as the Spaniard Suárez and the Dutchman Grotius. There was the successive elaboration of plans for securing international peace: in the seventeenth century, by Henry IV and his Huguenot Minister Sully, and by the English Quaker, William Penn; in the eighteenth, by the French Abbé Saint-Pierre and the German philosopher Immanuel Kant; in the early nineteenth, by the Englishman, Jeremy Bentham. Since then, we have had a proliferation of peace societies and peace foundations, and a multitude of peace activities sponsored by them, in which churches, and industrialists (like Carnegie and Nobel) and labor (including Socialists) have all participated. The modern peace movement, like the modern hospital movement, is a product of the West, and derives primarily from the West's religious teaching.

This is the basic inspiration, it seems to me, of Woodrow Wilson's absorption in creating a League of Nations and of Franklin Roosevelt's concern with establishing the present United Nations Organization. Both of these are unmistakable contributions of Western civilization, and whatever may be their shortcomings in the practical maintenance and furtherance of international peace, they do embody an ideal of peace which is indigenous to the West and which they serve to transmit to the world at large. Through them, despite what Russian and Chinese Communists may say or do, the Christian ideal and hope of peace remain.

5

To my way of thinking and from my knowledge of history, I feel confident that, despite occasional and sometimes very serious setbacks and perversions, our Western civilization has been historically characterized by a dynamic, progressive compassion in the broadest sense of the term. This includes not only the manifestations which I have here discussed, but also others, such as national self-determination, political and social democracy, and popular education, which I merely mention.

There is no doubt in my mind that our Western civilization has been marked by great eras of intellectual and cultural developments peculiarly enriching to itself and, through its outgoing dynamism, to the whole world. One was the medieval era of humanism; another has been the modern era of humanitarianism. Central to both, I believe, is the Christian conception of man and of man's godlike service to man.

The great big question of tomorrow is whether we can go onward in our progressive currents of liberty and plural authority and compassion, if we repudiate what chiefly set them in motion—Judaeo-Graeco-Christianity. Momentum gained from a past force may continue, we all know, after the force is withdrawn, but how long? How long after we turn from the Christian religion to embrace atheistic communism or pagan fascism shall we be able to retain those elements in our civilization which we now cherish?

In the present critical age, we need faith as perhaps never before, and faith not merely in ourselves or in an automatic progress. Progress is not automatic; it depends on human will and aspiration. Nor is change synonymous with progress; it may be retrogression. We in our age need renewed faith in God and in human brotherhood under God.

We also need Christian hope, to temper and supplant our present fears and our tendency to despair about what the present world is coming to. Hope and expectation of a better world should nerve us to put forth our best efforts for its attainment, and at the same time it should allay in us all undue suspicion about our fellows.

Above all we need charity—the *caritas* of Christ. Still most pertinent to our civilization is what the Apostle to the Gentiles wrote nineteen centuries ago: "Faith, hope, and charity persist, all three; but the greatest of them all is charity."